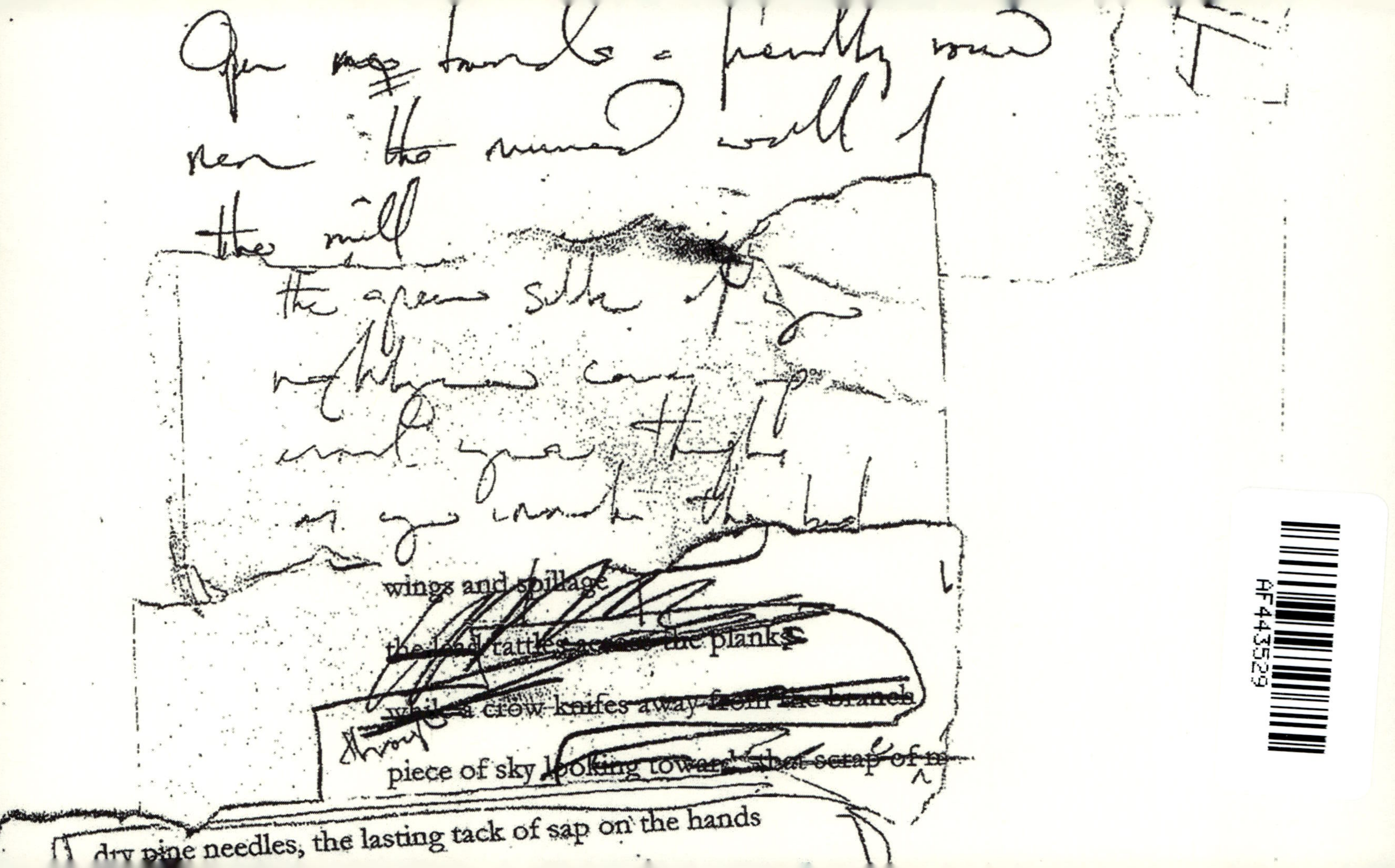

wings and spillage
the load rattles across the planks
while a crow knifes away from the branch
piece of sky looking toward that scrap of m
dry pine needles, the lasting tack of sap on the hands

tomato pl[...]

while I disintegrate behind them
viel

it a happiness
unspeakable by expression.

nothing and chimes
lapsed stanchion / [...]

while patio lights [...]
gloss, I rough green

for, if I will

INDIAN SUMMER RECYCLING

INDIAN SUMMER RECYCLING

NATHAN HAUKE

INDIAN SUMMER RECYCLING

THE MAGNIFICENT FIELD
Grand Rapids, Michigan

Published by The Magnificent Field

www.magnificentfield.com

ISBN 978-0-9981272-4-8

Cover art by Nick Francis Potter

Cover and interior design by Alban Fischer

Printed in the United States of America

First Edition

For Kirsten, Gus, and Frankie (in paradise)

Beauty is/ a defiance of authority

—WC Williams, *Paterson*

The conditions of composition, as of decomposition, are graphic . . . writing is clutter and debris; trace, husk, scar, sign, particle, element: bodily remains.

....

This subterranean density of copenetrating language and earth . . . is nonetheless all surface, a biodegradable strata of attention.

—J Rasula, *This Compost: Ecological Imperatives in American Poetry*

—————————————

I picked up two arrow-heads in the field beyond.

—HD Thoreau, *Journal* (Sept 28, 1851)

Contents

INDIAN SUMMER RECYCLING

Like a handsaw with a piece of black rag tied to the handle

Some people have it made and some people don't

Funny little dog named Pink ("Pank") playing in the street   near a blind corner
Metallic aftertaste of sunlight
Streaming through broken glass
Waking sawdust like smoke

Kid in the next room says, *It's a vampire*

How do you write ~~ghost~~ rusty flowers

Flecks of pollen eddy through the reflection

Shattered maiden fly glistens across the weed's shaft

Dark windows of the rickety barn

Where *X* hung himself

Thicket riddled with light

Thinking refractory garden after a hailstorm

Hole-punched leaves

A greasy rototiller wed to wakefulness

Smoothed under ash   wasted crowns

Last summer walking with Ely

Where were you while this summer was made?

Day swell (horsing around with a toy piano)

It's all in one ear
And out the other

....

We're hunkered down together   in weeds like killdeer
To be harrowed by heat   bleating through the irregularities of a web
To learn a song about old latticework
That's worn   dirty   full of holes
Corroded aluminum   pitched to weather headwinds
Verses a mangled roof   that wouldn't give

Kiss it goodbye

     A luminous
     Gold leaf
     Falling ` `

     Two beats
     After a sparrow

Red glass eye

Loose pollen
Water stain that darkens a streak near the vent
FANCY, a rough green door
Folk art made by folks for tourists
As opposed to the sun in a crushed hubcap
Knocks the wind out of you
A young mother picking lice out of her husband's hair in Sunshine Coin-Op
Bubbles caught up underneath a shard of burned window
Chaw-weed layers the charred paper target
Mint and fried-out blackberries
Clusters of moths shuffling back into the tree line

Ark

Turn the crank (music box)
I've got it bad
And that ain't good
Milky white sky buzzing in green
Sweet to the gristle
The way he should
Bent wobble of goat's beard in skunk water
Bees stunned by the crosshatching
While I nest in webbed rafters
While I black ant crossing through a paint stain

Sparrow says

Lay me down in the cemetery
Don't the lamb's quarter
Look wilted and tired
Don't the morning star
Look like a half-eaten cookie

Kids laughing across the street
And a glass of applejack
Remember to joy

Country music

Can't tell jumbled yellow rag moths from stray leaves

Stillness from the   totality of music (gone everywhere)

A songbird running on empty   *If my mother has to stay*

Before these Richie Rich condos crowd out the view

Tree's flattened mass swims a little right of the base   *In the nursing home much longer*

Relief or nostalgia of watching the old barn up the holler cave in

Stuck pixels arresting the material   *We might have to sell some of our land too*

(As an aside when his father isn't looking)

Tinder is a hatchet job

P/ *pR* / *rI*/ *iS*/ *sM*/ *mS*/ *s*

While light cuts into the layered stalks of weeds

A catechism poor as purple thistle

Wide distance from ash to black fur

Measured in countless thin yellow flowers

Silence a dusty hymnal

~~For love of music~~

Grown rich to the ears

As wind in a cross-pattern fence

Pink shred of ribbon tied to a branch near a deteriorating bottle cap

Where I piss into the brush

If somebody don't help me

Language
s Torn
Weathered
Screen
Dewy
Mosquitos
+++
Hatching
Tawny
Lamplight
Incomprehensible
As the smoldering husk
Of barn-
Hollowed dawn

Creation alone as each tree   folded within
The gleaming ordonnance of wide evergreen rows
Grief   you can't see the end of
Stray feathers   unsettled along the periphery
The rest is decomposition

Bury me deep

> *After Libby Cotten*

Honeybabe. Your eyes

Chirp a patch of Johnson weed

Reverberating through an overturned stove

Trash at the edge of a clearing   your eyes

Tadpoles swimming in tire ruts

Smell of mint   sweet clover

Widened by the heat

Honeybabe. Carves a lean arc

Away from the feeder

....

Current rises in pitch as stones etch bent glass

The tender flow of sap and aluminum shine

Windows cut into the barn like velvet

Where *X* hung himself after he lost all the family money

Honeybabe.

For a moment I thought

We were sharing

We weren't

Hurt or angry

Weeping willow

Bent under the weight of its leaves

Gnats swarming the screen

Would rather sleep than talk about the weather

Would rather not

Summer weeds dumbstruck by hearing

The long planks of our floor creak underfoot

Wakefulness more like a stammer

Wind chiseling textures of leaves into sunlight   *e c s t a c y*

____

Bitternut hickory shuddering after   *t e r r o r*

Little wind-up blackbird   shifts patiently
Stalk to stalk
Something in the back of my head
Like a horse fly
Darkness in the tree line
Collapses depth
Into black velvet
Sinking (as if to a "depth")
The sudden dullness of attention
No fizz

Leaves where light carves your eyes

Buoyed in bright debris of personality
Caught in rocks and roots all the way
Coughed up shards of glass
Meant to do better
Remembrance   a swollen hive
Crawling with bees
Wounds that won't close
Bleached cans of Natty Ice in the grass
Slick as a dented swing set

Bands of strata

S Howe: *Disorder is another order*

·ONE

Increasingly

Compact

Sense of

Circumstances

Childhood's   boarded-up window

Abandoned nest   stripped loops of thread

Old bricks   acoustic nodes distressed to weather

TWO

Verily it's the thought of salvation

Necessitates   salvation

Wrenching the lid open   to feel the serrated edge

The WORD OF ~~GOD~~   stricken in a hateful preacher's mouth

Certain to degrade   an unclaimed sparrow

THREE
Time

———————

Vocals

Buried under

The same three

Repeating chords

An eye is a dirty white bucket

Wedged in a pocket of roots

FOUR
A molted fawn   surfacing through ragwort near the bank
Picks its way toward   a wet black nexus of barbs below the trailer
Choral work as sunrise   eats the wood she disappears into

Walking out through

Blistered waves of feedback

Belief,

An occasion

Sure as goldenrod allergy

Sneaks up on you at the screen door

New River train

Oh darlin

  You can't love only one

And have any fun

Coffee bewilders

Torn bluets AHdorned by lampyridae

Religion: asking for the widest definition of presence

As elegy is glass turpentine rags to remember the dead

Crickets scrape and file a grave harmony

Knitting furrowed black over green

Until we can't tell patterned blades from crown

Truck lights sweep the road home

Into a haze of weeds and sweet clover

Momentum(s) as they pass

Thoreau: *I said to myself—I said to others*

Color is worse than eternity

Ribbons of water   shine like razor

Walking the dog   with a mouthful of blackberries

Rain leaves mirror everywhere

Trying not to   step in it

Thoreau: *Our life is a forgetting*

Where the bank of this shore erodes into current

ACME

For Keith

Wile E. Coyote builds a rocket-powered high-wire unicycle

Saws a trap door in a cliff that falls away   Etc.

....

Road Runner:

MEEP-MEEP. ZIP!   *BANG.*

Imperfection a generous precipice

ACME a piece of music   you loved to hear

Slanted aluminum streaked by matte gold leaves

Wet thorns by the creek   after a vision of F

Crumpling in shock   kicked by a horse at pasture

I woke up crying the day you died

Laid my hand on his chest to feel his ribs and make sure he was breathing

Hefted your ashes back into the church in a trance

Stupid to cleave to music   it changes

Learn to live with death it only

Grieves the living

Dog Creek

Like a sad dog's face in the window
You want to kiss it

You get lonely
When other people are sick

....

Spent firework in the grass   must have been some pretty thing
Micronutrients from decomposers   smolder like paths between trees
Concentrate on the electrostatic force   that holding the one you're on together
Hatchling insects   obscure the clarity of the riverbed

Can't help
The medium
Someone boarded over a window
Then   busted it up   *Tell you what*
Can't help
Someone   *I might say*
Who lives in that big condo   *You could*
Seeded rows   *Get*
Means the rich   *One of those*
Husband this garden too

                                                         Up at
                                                         Dog Creek

Thinking
A barn wall
Crawling with honeybees

        There's no reason

Shine an apple

You can hardly pick

Which record

Shines an apple

Will sharpen the needle

That ferries us

Toward the center

From one side/

To the other

Ceramic birds   crackle   near the handle

Oblivious to deer   we startle   from breakfast

It's hap   a bent corner post

Allows a body   into the cemetery

For rest   or winter grass

Where family names are   already

Worn off the stones

It's wild turkey scratch   around the roses

Ridge cross horses

Gallop wildly

To compass a

Turbulent center   manure and dust
Rise through a gauzy cloud of gnats
As ecstasy is duration
Alone at every shore
Mottled reflection of the black walnut
Repeating the deck's wet edge
Some things   you could see them forever
Means they've got you
Like a panicked rooster with its leg caught in a wire fence

After the parade

H Williams

("I Saw the Light")

Fiddle stomping

Goddamn joyful song

About the Civil War

Sun Drop Cola

Go seek some happy

Northern girl

For to be your wife

Chorus: *Three cheers for the Southern girls*

And the boys ~~they threw away~~

Rangy jack pines   homesick for your laugh

Little girl in orange chasing a rabbit across the grass

Calls a name that falls apart near the river

Time's a molting whippoorwill claps its wings

Song for the river Jordan: *Some of these days*   *(hallelujah)*

I'm going to sit down by my Jesus

EP's Garage

Yesterday
Dries sweet as wet hair
Spotted beech leaves
Rattle in turbulence overhead
Oceanic rhythm(s) of golden rod
Clear as bees move pollen
Back towards summer
Tattered glass
Crickets chirp
Through dull blue
Interior shell of an old truck
Oxidized near the pump
Pull down thy vanity
Reft of all
Save the weather
What's gotten into you?
....

F wags to play in the creek
Shaking with tenderness
Fogged wrapper in the flowers
Moths in chaw weed
A sea of love

Rapids gorged on purple phlox

Eggs and water racers in a clutch of mossy stones near the bank
Aluminum foil unearths dashed sun through weedy shallows
A grungy trailer with towels hanging in the windows
Smells like cat piss when wind catches the left corner of the field

Synthy glamour of a fountain at the mall
Brown glass and a car-keyed mess of silver
Tall grass   hair   wet ribbon
Tints that thread current
Before what you know to be true
Decays into the harmony

After Lucretius

Thank you with a raspberry seed in the hollow of my tooth

Gunshots up the ridge

For Mike

Bloom into handsome black mare

Miscreant neighbor kids   hack at the field's weedy border

With archaic golf clubs

Who was it told you   wasps drill right into the body of the cicada

Count yourself one   among so many blessings

A vessel to be filled and laid to waste

Wall of a burned-out condo   crumbling around what's left of the chimney

Falling is all edges

The sensation of falling

~~Mute in the grass~~

Thoreau: *Nothing*

In nature

Makes noise

Time composting   a toxic chicken house
Left to frame   wasted columns of smoky blue mirror
Mornings   after the industry dries up
Sweet clover and wild carrot
Mixed with honeysuckle   along the road
No one says you're healed   but you want to be
Addiction cleaves to the few twigs
Broken off   floating downstream

It's a family garden across the river

It's a coffee cup full of whiskey

Weather systems

("Today I feel like")

Point to the corresponding kitty face

On my t-shirt —>   the pixelated glare of cola

Dilates the pupils

Splintered green

Shotgun shells

In a bed of pine needles near the pasture

Mood wide as wild blue sheet plastic

Tacked by firewood

I was cemetery music—an idea

Collapsed into roots yarrow goosefoot chatter

Grass someone else sang to an unborn baby

A host of sparrows

Taken for

Another torqued

Constellation of barbs

Scatter that fence to

High heaven

Dry red flowers

A grown clamor against the rail can you heal the dead

Let them go

Cicadas throwing nets over each other

In a brood of shadows by LITTLE ANGELS OF HEAVEN

Tracing an origin that moves toward the foreground

From a gaudy reflector near the cemetery gate

A hummingbird frozen in purple phlox

Frees itself to peel rhythmic strips from the eaves

Green rain barrel

Green leaves and a tangled leash

Muddy shit shovel

Flotsam   seeds

F's panting

Wants a pretzel

Gets one

It's a horse

Honeybabe. That piece that looks like a horse
Delicious stars almond puff pastry
While Ruby pants through heat near the stairs
Honeybabe. Goldfinch magnet
Voice medium blue truck full of garbage
Ten seconds from a meltdown
Wants chewing gum
Honeybabe. Irises musty rot
Runny green salsa
Calls you on the phone or what
The road steaming all the way home

Leftovers

Moth eaten stones

Loosed from the old dam wall

Into the withered grandeur of ragwort

WE WERE YOUNG TOGETHER   a fishing boat tied to the dock

Is suddenly untethered and pushed out into current

Dull glint of tinsel near the tree dump

As money flowers or doesn't flower in a stranger's wallet

....

Clash on the radio

Pretty blue

Hint of movement

Where condensation frays a chalky edge

Into peripheral green blur

As devil's mischief

May produce beautiful gardens

Standing slack-jawed

Breathless as a stomped pop can

Swarmed by gnats

At the tender approach

Of the starving fawn

With a Snoopy

Dog collar

Tightened

Around its neck

/

Summer thunderstorm

A skirt that swells around your waist   before it falls

Slick yellow goldfinches crumbling their branches

Thinking you can't be present

To the palm against your shoulder

Melody and drag of desire   truncated by distances

Coming around the corner of one feeling into another

Crickets interminable chirping beneath the deck

Trying   to

Push   down   anger
That   shakes   dirty foam in an eddy
How angry
Depends on   the extent
To which we live
Hand to mouth   it's exhausting
To dream your animal face
Sweating behind the death mask
While bees   crawl out around your collar
To be   unrecognizable
To yourself   friends

Voices
From a boat radio
Mostly static
Bouncing through
Early AM swell of waves
Moldered electrical wires
Below the helm
America: a vision
Where paint
Chips up off
The idea

A piece of string in the leaves

Green leak of treatment out of softening boards

Buoy made from an empty bottle of detergent

Rough strip of moonlight pasted over the end of the dock

Surface tension of the face in the mirror

As you close the medicine cabinet

:: Turn towards the ones you love

Before Eosphoros turns your eyes into ash

Talk along the river

To think of you alone
("To think of
You alone")
Beagles at the beagle farm
Howl something dreadful
Children screaming
Bloody murder
Daylight chiseling trees
Into scuffed violets
Couldn't tell
Who it was
Siphoned that gas
Out of
The farm pump

The living and the dead
Talk
Along the river
Stillness
Pierced by
Intricate
Outcroppings of
Wild carrot

To think of you alone

("To think of
You alone")   Talk
                        Along the river
Back again
For a fix
Same as a hummingbird
Drawn to
Wet leaves for sugar

I let the names of loved ones fill me
Took a deep breath
Across the lip of the bottle

Stones garbled beneath current

Bright red stones thrumming under milky glass
Temper the wind-scuffed drone of a dented panel
Before the medium scatters it
Angular black snails stuck to the slick edge
Gnats swarming through the weedy border
Old barn where *X* hung himself
Moss gathers in roots along the bank
Stamina like bubbles of foam disintegrating on the surface

Dusting

With a strip

Torn from beloved

Beach towel

Glossy yellow threads of leaves jumble rag moths

Swell of instruments tuning through chatter

The way K carries F's fur out to birds for their nests

Before she takes your hand and pulls you through one room/ voice into another

Greasy white feathers of current slide over tarry shadows of trees

Coolness of fall gathers in the floorboards

Under the left side of your face

Snow falling into a mirror four years ago

Forgotten on a porch in a neighborhood that felt like home

Sleeper

Your eyes

      Tall

Grass

      Torn

Wild

      Car   *Crumpled*

                Laughter

                Near

ROT   *Labrador*

                Thermometer

Bruised webbing
Sewn through an old satellite dish
Across the trampoline

Beast that
Scratches the aluminum door
To be let back into the house
When the storm turns windows into mirror

Bleached roots
Below the watermark
Shirt's wet around the waist
From your blue swimsuit
You were going to change
You fell asleep in

Hammer

Splinters of color hammered through LORD

Hail   cuts leaves with precision

Gerrids carve   a shaky panel of sky

Across the wreckage   of a derelict stove

Quartered below New River

Physics

All I'm saying is

      It takes a certain amount of electricity

To regrow a bone

Broke a window in the flowerbed
And oozed in through a crawlspace under the house
Nosing a leathery snail with a fractured shell under wet leaves
Blamed the dealers who lived across the dirt road from the trailer
No one was worried about the stuff that was stolen
They were worried about the guns (heirlooms)
Shattered glass amber in memory
Glitters like an old toy in a wooden box

———————————

You leave it for the next one comes along

A beetle in the screen

Marbled leaves with vibrant edges
Move lines through the reflection of a room you stood in
To spread blankets across the floorboards
Raw as cut eyes in a fog of pollen
ECSTASY   the length of a drowned tree
Smoothed by debris of like occasions

Waiting the appropriate amount of time for music = forever
A long 4x4 in the creek bed rotting emerald

Saying *Jesus*

ONE

A cube of sugar

Melting in a horse's mouth

The hairy lower branches   snag chromatic braids of water
Pine pollen slurry   tremors relieved to momentum
Hours after Eryn and Brenda   try to help a katydid stuck in the rug
Flimsy silver leaf   caught up near tangle of minnows
Carved by noise and the desire to be changed
Name place gauged in wood   like a blowtorch cutting through fog

TWO
K says
Our wedding song
Otis Redding's "Cigarettes and Coffee"

Bunny Scout triptych

ONE
Neighbors

The neighbors are letting the boy
Stay alone in the trailer another dog
Sister gone to foster care
Home again now too?
Feral children isolated by
Three generations
Classic sun-bleached plastic Santa
Tangled in razor briar
Jumpy strung-out addict
Mom bipolar grandmother
Housebound great grandmother's cats
Clawing tattered white curtains for daylight ///

TWO
3/28

Pits of
Your eyes

In the
Ultra

Sound

Your ears

Swimming

Between

Two pulses

THREE

Triangles

Slanted across grubby tile

Cartoon rabbits trying to earn Bunny Scout badges fishing at the laundry mat

Catch an old boot and cut to commercial   magic happens

Colored sheets uneven momentum *THUMPF(s)*

Oval suds near an empty bag of Bugles

Ambient bleed of recess lighting above scooped sitting area

Where buds pattern mirror to garden a blank wall

While a handsome grey rabbit laughs spinning in a tire swing

:: See you around, Max

A dog wrings the neck for gladness

INDIAN SUMMER RECYCLING

STALLION BELT BUCKLE

Dry leaves in grainy heat startled like a toy duck with a shredded orange bill

Time abandoned to eternity   a knot unraveling

Melody that disintegrates through the same old fucked speaker

A dog wrings the neck for gladness

INDIAN SUMMER RECYCLING

STALLION BELT BUCKLE

Dry leaves in grainy heat startled like a toy duck with a shredded orange bill

Following a path

Into a copse

Of moss-scraped beeches

That's been   shot up with light

We cleave to occasions   teach me dissolution

Desire(s)   foam disintegrating

                    In current

....

A part of and apart from
What's eating us

Can't map   the gospel of a crow's *caw*
Because I'm a loose arrangement of maple keys falling
Thistle that peels up out of the plaster of paris

I've seen orange ribbon tied to a blue window
Thunderheads troubling the clover
A wolfish girl with sticks in her hair
Wearing a stretched-out t-shirt that reads   *I didn't slap you*

I high-fived your face

Long gone lonesome

      ONE

      A saw aches

We set our teeth   against attachments

Corroded as music   (which is our body)

Ragwort (which is our body)

Reflecting ragwort an answer

Where mirror breaks up into current

TWO

Ragwort

Love what's gone

Ahead into new noise and affection

Seek ye first the kingdom

And be glad in it, ETC.

Layered reverberations

Of childhood hymns

In dewy webbing near the bank

Fill the hollow of my mouth

Radio

The sweat-streaked sky's blurred ambience
Bakes crazy mud   radiant patterns in red hawk feathers
While bleached light knifes through weeds and mirror
Chewed mint near the ditch
Swatting gnats away from your legs
Pungent smell of hot garbage
At the recycling center   sans lilac

To shatter the brown bottles
Then, the green ones   means a kindness
As a stomped box
Reminds an enclosure to music

Pastoral (years later)

Heaven is

The perception

Of Heaven

Tires laid across the trailer roof to weight and quiet wind
Crusted brown cows huddled together for warmth in the corner of the field
Munching grass blue blankets for horses
Near the factory parking lot
Particular natural facts are ~~signs of~~
Particular spiritual facts
Leaning across the table with your flannel shirt buttoned low
Beneath the truss of the old mill   my eyes
Iridescent minnows wobbling in a bucket
A hiccup in the melody
Means the pleasure of hearing it again

Another

Patternless

Pattern of excitement

Dull green ribbon past its prime

A cacophony of color

Bubbling up pleated yellow leaves in the gutter

One vision is a slick window another

Beard of bees threading burst pussy willow

Intentions, a handful of twigs snapped over the knee

Plastic Fanta bottle in the ditch

Salt-stained aluminum that glints near pasture

....

Name is a gift

Malleable as mud

Where chips of mirror slur

Under the horse's hooves

After music the music of chimes and kerosene

3/16
John 3:16

Reckoning
A shed's fract/
ured truss
Pinned to
Thrown
Corrugated
Tin sheet

An eye   a
Dirty
White
Buck-
Et
Wedged in a   pocket of roots
Made to catch   whatever
Redeemed by   shadows of budded branches
That drift   over a column on the floor
Another current   muted by a smudged surface
Trash strewn   deck of the trailer

Crab apple's gnarled branches

Distance incommensurate in the cracked mirror

Calendar like a crooked row of nails sheens in a clamor

Men with rifles don't cotton to strangers

I myself am becoming

Dead June bug in the lawn chair's cup holder

Sagged splintered wicker

Harried dandelions

Tangle of chimes steaming at the rail

Crimson wounds the eyes to cut an opening for autumn

You throw a stone scatters the reflection

We used to say

Now you're a tadpole

The size of an orange seed

For G

Knots in our floor
Worn by joyful noise of your arrival

Your mother read library books in the tub
We paid bills and tried not to think
How much we needed x where the money would come from
Hunkered down under a thrift store lamp   near the kerosene heater
Some days like a horse chewing on a fence
Got some brightness in its coat
Hollow bulbs of ice that gather in the roots of a half-frozen stream
Your birth was animal   your mother's face blurred behind patterned glass
I tried to offer water from tile nearby
Wide moment   before the stunned first feathers of your cries filled the room

Spectral glare

SONNE

As a green bottle shatters the light

Snow glitter sandpapers the eyes:: LOOK

Beads of melt seeping through the bottom of a blue trampoline

A porous edge collects honey

A current

Sweeping dead grass into a frenzy   **Bruises the sky**

Melody you love   comes to surface

And you've got a friend on the line

Hornet sewing violets   through the deck rail

Rack of green near the post   black-eyed susans

LITTLE ANGELS OF HEAVEN

Prismatic condensation in the hummingbird feeder

Rhododendron thriving by the compost

Moss flecked bark   laundry detergent

Yes, my clumsy bird at tree's edge

Morning buzz through a worn-out speaker   might be a bad connection

Leaves strain through shifting tracks of wind

Rabbit ears have a mind of their own

Hearing a tangle of wild roses

Pattern of days that drifts through static

Heat-shocked field grass

Dull brown sheet metal   transfigured by rust

G, the next place

Trembling across the surface of your eyes

Notes

Thanks to dear friends and family for all the company, especially Kirsten Jorgenson, Gus, and Frankie.

Shout outs to Connor Childers, Colleen Choate, Shira Dentz, Chris Dunsmore, Emilie Enzmann, Martha Enzmann, Olivia Fitts, Evan Gray; my folks, Doug and Lanora Hauke; Josh Hauke, Sarah Hauke, Emilie Kerscher, Hank Lazer, Sam Lineberger, Doug Little; The old Mercantile Crew: Jim, Jack (in paradise), and Walt; Gina Myers, Andy Nicholson, Nick Francis Potter, Ruby (in paradise), Brenda Sieczkowski, Ely Shipley, Mike Sikkema, Lyn Soeder, Tom Sternal (in paradise), and Jen Tynes.

Thank you to *Poets in Need* for help when we really needed it.

Thanks to folks who made music I listened to while I was writing: Dirty Beaches, Liz Harris/Grouper, Aaron Martin, Sean McCann, Mountains, Mick Turner and Will Oldham (individually and in concert as Marquis de Tren and Bonny Billy), Gillian Welch.

INDIAN SUMMER RECYCLING riffs on strangers' t-shirts and conversational flotsam alongside lines/lyrics/ideas from many others that were drawn into its compost: Elizabeth ("Libby") Cotten, Bob Dylan, John Lee Hooker, Robert Johnson, John Milton, Otis Redding, Max and Ruby (annoying cartoon in the laundry mat), Nina Simone, Hank Williams, etc.

More specifically, the phrase "patternless pattern of excitement" comes from Ten Berrigan's *The Sonnets* ("Another patternless pattern of attention"). The lines "particular natural facts are ~~signs of~~/ Particular spiritual facts" represent an edit of Ralph Waldo Emerson's *Nature* and attempt to demarcate a primary difference between Emerson and Henry David Thoreau. The title "Color is worse than eternity" comes from Robert Smithson's "Incidents of Mirror-Travel in The Yucatan." The assertion that "disorder is another order" comes from Susan Howe's *The Birth-*

mark: unsettling the wilderness in American literary history ("Bands of strata"). The line "Babe, I couldn't do nothin' until I got myself unwound" is from Robert Johnson's "Dead Shrimp Blues." The command to "Pull down thy vanity" is from Ezra Pound's *Pisan Cantos* ("EP's garage"). The following lines are drawn from Thoreau's *Journal:* "I said to myself—I said to others" ("New River train"), "Our life is a forgetting" ("Color is worse than eternity"), "Nothing in nature makes noise" ("Falling is all edges").

Acknowledgments

Many thanks to Jen Tynes and Mike Sikkema at Horse Less Press for publishing a number of these poems in the chapbook *Honeybabe, Don't Leave Me Now* (2013). Thanks also to Mike Sikkema at Shirt PocketPress for publishing "Pastoral (years later)" as a mini-chapbook with sketches by Kate Kern Mundie (2013).

Thanks to Abe Smith and Shelly Taylor for including "Like a handsaw with a piece of black rag tied to the handle," "Tinder is a hatchet job," "Leftovers," "Crab apple's gnarled branches," "Red glass eye," "After Lucretius," and "Pastoral (years later)" in *Hick Poetics* (Lost Roads Press, 2015). Abe also kindly featured "After Lucretius" at Lost Roads/ Lines.

"Tinder is a hatchet job," "Gunshots up the ridge," "Bunny Scout triptych," "Dusting // With a strip // Torn from beloved," and "Another // Patternless / Pattern of excitement" were finalists for CutBank's Patricia Goedicke Prize (2014).

Thanks too to the editors of the following journals in which these poems appeared:

4ink7: An Unction from the Holy One
"After music"
"Gunshots up the ridge"
"Tinder is a hatchet job"
"Physics"

Banango Street:
"Bunny Scout triptych"
"Trying to"

Coconut:
"New River train"
"Leftovers"
"Following a path / Into a copse / Of moss-scraped beeches"

Country Music:

"Another // Patternless / Pattern of excitement"

Denver Quarterly:

"Sleeper"

"Spectral glare"

Dusie:

"Bury me deep"

"After Lucretius"

"Wakefulness more like a stammer"

"It's a horse"

"Shine an apple"

E-Ratio:

"Leaves where light carves my eyes"

"Saying *Jesus*"

Interim:

"Long gone lonesome"

"A beetle in the screen"

"Radio"

"Weather systems / (Today I feel like)"

"If somebody don't help me"

"Walking out through // Blistered waves of feedback"

"Dog Creek"

"Talk along the river"

"To think of you alone"

The Laurel Review:

"Ridge cross horses"

"Red glass eye"

Momoware:

"Stones garbled beneath current"

P r o j e c t o r:

"ACME" ·

[65]

Reality Beach:

"Bands of strata"

"Hammer"

"We used to say // Now you're a tadpole // The size of an orange seed"

Real Poetik:

"Color is worse than eternity"

Spork:

"Falling is all edges"

"A piece of string in the leaves"

"After the parade"

Witness

"As devil's mischief / May produce beautiful gardens"

Zen Monster:

"EP's Garage"

Nathan Hauke is also the author of *Every Living One* (Horse Less Press, 2015), *In the Marble of Your Animal Eyes* (Publication Studio, 2013), and four chapbooks. His poems have been anthologized in *Hick Poetics* (Lost Roads Press, 2015) and *The Arcadia Project: North American Postmodern Pastoral* (Ahsahta Press, 2012).

wings and spillage
the load rattles across the planks
while a crow knifes away from the branch
piece of sky looking toward that scrap of n
dry pine needles, the lasting tack of sap on the hands

until it disintegrates behind them
veil

it a happiness
unexplained by experience.

nothing and chimes
lapped strokes of touch

until patio lights tremble
glow through green

for it will
then